DIRECTOR'S CHOICE

ENGLISH HERITAGE

DIRECTOR'S CHOICE

Simon Thurley

ENGLISH HERITAGE

SCALA

INTRODUCTION

WHEN I BECAME CHIEF EXECUTIVE of English Heritage in 2002 I thought I knew the great collection of buildings and monuments in its care quite well. I had been visiting them since I was a young child and a year never went by without notching up another few sites. But I soon realised that I can't have seen more than about 30 of the total of 409, and set off on an odyssey to see every one of them. It took me three years; the last to be ticked off the list was the amphitheatre in Cirencester, in the gloom and drizzle of a November evening in 2005.

The 409 sites in England are in fact just a part of the extraordinary total of 880 sites and monuments collected by the British government after 1882. The others are now in the care of CADW and Historic Scotland, the organisations that inherited responsibility for them in 1984 and 1991 respectively. The 1882 Ancient Monuments Act was an important, but limited, measure. Included within it was a list of 68 ancient monuments – the very first places to be conserved by the State for the good of the nation. The act established a principle that was to be built upon in 1913 with a second Act of Parliament, which was the beginning of a process that continued energetically to the 1960s – that of identifying and assembling the most important national monuments into a collection run for the benefit of all. In this book I will give a glimpse into this story through the sites that I think tell it best.

In 1913 great national monuments were regarded as documents – structures that could be read and interpreted like manuscripts to reveal the hidden truths of Britain's story. The Victorians believed in collecting, categorising and displaying artefacts for the advancement of human knowledge, and for public edification. As sites came into national ownership they were stripped of their overgrowth, relieved of piles of fallen masonry and presented not as romantic ivy-clad ruins but as pristine documents to be read by the public like text books.

The government inspectors of Ancient Monuments developed a collecting policy that aimed at capturing what they regarded as the most significant national sites. Places that could not immediately be acquired were listed for future consideration. These included sites still in military use, such as Berwick Barracks, Dover Castle and Pendennis Castle, all of which were handed over once their active service was over. Battles were picked carefully and mostly won. For example, when the Forestry Commission planned to plant trees over the top of the Neolithic flint mines at Grime's Graves shortly after the First World War the inspectors stepped in and acquired the site from under the Commission's nose. Private owners were an important part of the story too. Perhaps the most notable gift was that of Cecil Chubb and his wife who, in 1916, donated Stonehenge to the nation.

After the war the political consensus that lay behind the assemblage of a national heritage collection collapsed. The National Trust henceforth took the country houses, and the government resisted calls from the inspectors to collect other types of heritage. In 1983, in order to gather together in a single organisation all the state's responsibilities for heritage protection, English Heritage was created. An important part of its new mission was to make the National Heritage Collection in England more profitable and enjoyable. Its first chairman, Edward, Lord Montagu, established a membership scheme based on that of the National Trust. Today over one million people have signed up.

The fledgling English Heritage recognised that its collection was hardly a representative slice of the national story, being heavily weighted to abbeys, castles and prehistoric monuments – buildings seen as being most important before the war. The first two chairmen sought to redress the balance. The freehold of Brodsworth Hall, left to the nation in 1986, brought a great Victorian country house to the collection; Down House added a site of huge historical significance in 1996; and Wrest Park came to English Heritage in 2006, securing one of England's most important and beautiful landscapes.

While English Heritage today occasionally adds to the collection, most recently with the spectacular Harmondsworth Barn in 2011, we feel that it is better, wherever possible, for other bodies to secure the future of our great monuments. We, however, continue to care for those that we have in our care and to open them for people to enjoy and appreciate, just as was intended by our founders in Queen Victoria's reign.

Boxgrove Quarry

Britain's earliest human remains

Chichester, West Sussex

SOME 500,000 YEARS AGO Boxgrove lay below tall chalk cliffs on a fertile coastal plain, home to lions, hyenas, bears, rhinoceros, elephants, horses and giant deer. These animals attracted our ancestors, *Homo heidelbergensis,* who camped here, probably around a spring or water hole, making flint tools with which to kill, butcher and eat their prey. In 1993 the remains of two of these people were discovered, then the earliest human bones found in Europe, and still the oldest yet found in Britain. Their living environment was perfectly preserved, undisturbed for some five hundred millennia. Objects lay where they had been discarded; flakes of flint rested where they had fallen; and animal bones close by told of how groups sat around carcasses as they were prepared. Boxgrove quarry is, in fact, the largest undisturbed area of Lower Palaeolithic land surface in Europe.

Such a site is obviously of supreme importance for British archaeology, but after 20 years of excavation by the Institute of Archaeology in London it was clear to English Heritage that it could not be protected in the normal way. This is because scheduling, the most effective form of legal protection for an archaeological site, requires a structure or man-made feature to be identified, and no such thing existed at Boxgrove. As a result, in May 2003 English Heritage bought the quarry as the most effective way of securing its future.

The archaeological trenches were backfilled and, after some remedial works, the quarry was relandscaped. There is nothing to see on the site today, but thanks to English Heritage ownership our successors now have the opportunity to find out more about the earliest humans on this land.

Grimes Graves

Vast Neolithic industrial site

Thetford, Norfolk

IN THE EXTENSIVE COLLECTION of guidebooks on my shelves, the one from Grimes Graves has a special place. It is the first one I ever acquired, bought for me in 1969 by my aunt who had taken me there in the school holidays. Grimes Graves is a vast Neolithic flint mine with over 300 shafts covering an area of 16 acres. Its heyday was probably between 3000BC and 1900BC.

The shafts are wide, around 12 metres in diameter, presumably to allow light to penetrate to the bottom, some 14 metres below. From the base of the shaft, tunnels, or galleries, were dug outwards like the spokes of a wheel, using pickaxes made from antlers. A couple of the shafts are open to the public and, though these days people are not allowed to crawl along the galleries, the sensation of being far down a Neolithic mine is amazing.

The deepest seams were full of black, shiny, flawless flint – really desirable stuff that would be roughly shaped on the surface and then traded far afield where it would be trimmed and polished into tough sharp blades of the highest quality. To run a mine like this there had to be a skilled labour force, a constant supply of pre-pared timber for scaffolding, ropes, buckets, shovels and a continuous supply of antler picks. Grimes Graves reveals the sophistication of society 5,000 years ago.

At least 28 mines have been excavated since 1852, and the site as a whole was taken into guardianship by the Commissioners of Works in May 1932, having been wrested from the arms of the Forestry Commission, who originally wanted to cover the area with a huge spruce wood to help solve the acute timber shortage after the First World War. Later that same month the site opened to the public for the first time, and it has been open ever since.

Silbury Hill and West Kennet Long Barrow

Ancient living landscape

Avebury, Wiltshire

MANY THOUSANDS OF PEOPLE every year go inside West Kennet Long Barrow, one of the largest and best preserved burial chambers in Britain. Many fewer have been right into the centre of Silbury Hill 30 metres below the mound. This is what I had the privilege to do in 2007 as English Heritage conducted an emergency operation to stabilise the hill, which had been weakened by centuries of speculative burrowing.

The Roman invasion of AD43 stands less than halfway in time between the building of Silbury Hill and the present day. Its origins, purpose and meaning have been lost in the depths of time, but we do know that it and West Kennet Long Barrow were components of a huge ceremonial landscape linked with the nearby stone circle at Avebury. The 2007 excavation showed that the hill grew in phases and was made of soils from different places, perhaps brought by people from settlements who wanted to associate themselves with the hill.

A number of long barrows were built in the vicinity of Silbury, the largest being the close-by barrow at West Kennet. We don't know exactly what these were used for either. Many were used for burial at some point, but it is very likely that they had a ceremonial purpose perhaps connected with the emerging agricultural economy.

Both the long barrow and the mound were included on the original schedule of monuments of 1882, and when they were put up for sale in 1873 they were bought by Sir John Lubbock, the promoter of the original Ancient Monuments Act. Lubbock, determined to lead by example, immediately put them in the guardianship of the Ancient Monuments Board. When he was eventually awarded a peerage he took the title Lord Avebury.

Stonehenge

The world's most famous prehistoric monument

Amesbury, Wiltshire

STONEHENGE IS THE ONLY STRUCTURE in the United Kingdom that is instantly recognisable worldwide. It belongs to a select group of places that have a meaning for people all over the world, but exactly what it was, how it was used or what it means is still a subject of controversy and speculation.

Its very fame ensured that saving Stonehenge for the nation became a crusade, and it was one of the monuments to be placed on the Schedule of the 1882 Act. In 1915, after years of wrangling, it was sold amid fears that its new owner would limit access or even dismantle the monument and sell it. However, the purchasers, Cecil Chubb and his wife, reassured everyone, and in 1918 (after three years of opening it to the public themselves) they gifted the entire monument to the nation.

Stonehenge was a sacred landscape used for ceremonies in which death rituals and the movements of the sun played a part. Thus it is part mausoleum, part ceremonial arena whose use morphed and developed over a period of 5,000 years. People lived amidst the monuments, and in the last few years we have found the remains of their robust little square houses. So the Stonehenge landscape was a busy, inhabited place – not the gaunt, deserted plain that we see today.

Once a year, at the Summer Solstice, we invite people into the centre of the stone circle to see the midsummer sun rise. I have seen the sun come over the horizon on a couple of occasions. As its beams fill the circle and people clap and cheer, dance and sing, I'm never quite sure why, but I feel that I'm somewhere immensely special and that I'm witnessing something that transcends time.

Chysauster

Perfect Iron Age village

Penzance, Cornwall

THE LITTLE TIMBER SHOP and ticket office at Chysauster sells
green rubber grass snakes. For 1,700 years snakes were the
only inhabitants of this remarkable deserted village. After
being abandoned in the third century it was only properly
rediscovered by the founding father of Cornish archaeology, William Borlase, in 1873. Borlase started excavating the
village huts but the first large-scale dig didn't take place
until 1928, revealing a settlement of at least nine home-
steads of a type only found in the Land's End peninsula
and the Scilly Isles. The owner of the site, Colonel C. R. R.
Malone, promptly presented it to the nation.

The houses are grouped together in what is sometimes
called England's oldest surviving village street. Each was
built around a courtyard off which were a number of robust
little rooms probably thatched with reed and built of carefully fitted granite blocks. One room was the living room,
the rest may have been bedrooms. Each house had its own
little garden in which vegetables may have been grown. The
landscape around the settlement has probably changed little since the Roman occupation during which it was built.
Fields growing grain would have surrounded the village,
and livestock such as pigs and goats would have roamed the
central street.

Chysauster village sits in the shadow of a great Iron Age
hill fort. What we do not understand is the relationship
between the two. Did the occupants of the village flee to the
hill fort in times of trouble? Was it where they worshipped
and traded? Or was the hill fort occupied by an overlord to
whom the villagers owed tribute or rent?

Maiden Castle

Europe's largest Iron Age hill fort

Dorchester, Dorset

AMONGST THE MANY GREAT TREASURES in the care of English Heritage Maiden Castle is amongst the most spectacular. It is the largest and most complex Iron Age hill fort in Europe. General Pitt Rivers recognised it as being one of the top priorities for our predecessors at the Office of Works as early as 1889, and it was passed from the Duchy of Cornwall and presented to the nation in 1908.

Maiden was never a castle in the sense that we might use the word to describe a medieval fort. It was a town, for within its ramparts lived a considerable population. At its peak the inhabitants lived in uniformly designed circular houses laid out in an orderly manner. People baked bread, spun wool and wove cloth; grain was stored and ground; antler and bone was worked. They wore jewellery, rode horses and used coin to trade; they buried their dead in a cemetery and built their own ritual buildings. Maiden was a wealthy and successful place to live. This is reflected in its size and in the grandeur of its defences. At its peak it enclosed 47 acres, the size of 50 football pitches, and was surrounded by three banks and two ditches. We should never doubt that although these ramparts were for show, they served a genuine defensive purpose. Large stores of slingshots have been found, revealing that the residents were ready to defend their homes if they had to.

When the Romans came the place was abandoned as a settlement and Durnovaria (modern Dorchester) was established. Yet Maiden retained significance and the Romans built a square temple with a mosaic floor, a house for its priest and a circular shrine in the middle of the fort. The remains of these are the only ones now visible on site.

Richborough Roman Fort

England's most impressive Roman walls

Sandwich, Kent

IT SEEMS VERY LIKELY that Richborough was the place where the Emperor Claudius's troops landed in Britain in AD43. Forty years later, around AD85, it was decided to build a colossal triumphal arch there. This was around 25 metres tall, clad with Italian white marble and adorned with engaged columns and pilasters. There is no doubt that this was meant to be a ceremonial gateway to Britain, possibly celebrating the successful completion of the campaigns of Agricola as well as Claudius's initial invasion.

The arch is now gone, although fragments of it can be seen embedded in the third-century walls that presently surround the site. These walls are one of the most impressive remains of the Roman occupation in the whole of Britain. Over 3 metres wide at their base, and rising to a height of 8 metres, the walls were not simply a piece of brutal military engineering: they were given a decorative appearance by the disposition of different coloured stones. The north elevation of the north wall still retains a chequerboard pattern.

The massive Roman walls made the excavation of Richborough an obvious priority for the Office of Works, and the site was placed into guardianship in October 1912. Between 1922 and 1938 the Office of Works funded J. P. Bushe-Fox and B. W. Pearce to piece together its history. The excavations were boosted by the employment of large numbers of people who had lost their jobs during the Great Depression. As the excavators revealed the history of the site, so the Ministry bought more land and, in 1929, the neighbouring landowner handed over the adjacent Roman amphitheatre.

Lullingstone Roman Villa

400 years of Roman high-life
Eynsford, Kent

ALTHOUGH A STORM IN 1939 turned up pieces of mosaic in the roots of a fallen tree, excavations at Lullingstone were delayed until 1949 by the advent of war. Digging continued until 1961, involving a great number of local people. The Ministry of Works (successor to the Office of Works) took over care of the site in 1956 and, together with Kent County Council, rerouted a road that lay over some of the remains. It was officially brought into guardianship in 1958 and a roof was thrown over the whole thing in 1963.

Perhaps the most important aspect of this well-preserved and extensive villa is that people were established on the site before the Roman invasion and continued to live there after the legions had left. The long period of inhabitancy throws light on changing lifestyles during the Roman occupation. The owners of the villa were rich and fashionable, and built and extended their house in the latest Roman style, with additions such as a bathing complex and landscaped gardens containing a shrine. One of the marble busts found on site perhaps suggests that the villa was once the country home of the Governor of Britannia, Publius Helvius Pertinax, later briefly Emperor of Rome.

By the second half of the fourth century this pagan shrine was converted into one of the earliest surviving Christian chapels in England and at least part of the villa became a house-church. It was abandoned in the early fifth century. Although some of the best finds are now in the British Museum, the villa and its collections bring to life in an extraordinary way upper-class life in Roman Britannia.

Housesteads

Vercovicium, Britain's most important Roman Fort

Hexham, Northumberland

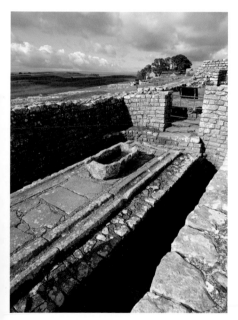

IN THE AUTUMN OF 2006 I walked the length of Hadrian's Wall, an extraordinary and exhilarating experience. Nothing prepares you for the wildness and beauty of the central section and nothing anywhere in northern Europe is quite like Housesteads, one of 12 forts constructed along the line of the wall. Thanks to the efforts of generations of archaeologists and, from 1951, the Ministry of Works, it is the most extensive and best preserved of any Roman frontier fort.

It survives in an extraordinary state of preservation, complete with walls, four gateways, towers, barracks, hospital, granaries, the commanding officer's house and, a source of endless fascination to visitors, the latrines. Although Housesteads contains some of the best-preserved Roman buildings in Britain, it also retains one of only two civilian settlements (the *vicus*) to have been excavated on the northern frontier. As well as domestic and public buildings the *vicus* contained shops, workshops and taverns.

The fort, which covers 2.2 hectares, would have housed a garrison of 800 men, the first regiment of Tungrians, recruited, in the main, from modern Belgium. The *vicus* became a substantial little settlement supplying the garrison with food, drink and entertainment.

The Ministry of Works had long wanted to take the whole of Hadrian's Wall into guardianship, and gradually moved to negotiate section by section with an array of landowners. Because Housesteads was already owned by the National Trust it was not seen as a priority case, but nonetheless the Ministry of Works took it into care in 1951. The whole wall was never secured by the Ministry and its ownership remains fragmented amongst over a hundred landowners.

Tintagel Castle

*Dark Age fortress and legendary
home of King Arthur*

Tintagel, Cornwall

WHILST KING ARTHUR IS LEGEND, the dramatic remains of Tintagel Castle are real and tangible parts of Dark Age history. We don't know who made their headquarters in this wild and impregnable spot in the years after the withdrawal of the Roman legions but we do know that the settlement there was wealthy, successful and cosmopolitan. Mediterranean pottery and glass have been excavated on the site dating from between the fifth and seventh centuries.

Before the site was appropriated by Richard, Earl of Cornwall in the thirteenth century, and a new castle was built there, Tintagel was already associated with both King Arthur and Tristan and Isolde. Indeed it may have been the historical associations of the place that encouraged Richard to start the construction of the castle in 1233. By the Tudor period the castle was in a state of dilapidation, although it was refortified as part of the attempt to repel the Spanish Armada. Today, Tintagel Castle remains in the possession of the Duke of Cornwall (Prince Charles), although it was passed into the guardianship of the Office of Works in 1931.

Showing the castle to nearly 200,000 visitors a year inevitably balances people's interest in legend with the archaeological and historical facts. But in telling history as we understand it, nobody would want to de-romanticise such a magical place, especially as we know that during the Dark Ages Tintagel was indeed the residence of an important overlord. What his name was, or where he came from, though, remains unknown.

Lindisfarne Priory

Holy site of early Christianity

Berwick-Upon-Tweed, Northumberland

ALTHOUGH THE ROMANTIC RUINS of Lindisfarne Priory on Holy Island retain the power to evoke the mysteries of early English Christianity the remains that we see today date from its early twelfth-century refoundation. The first timber structures erected by monks sent from Iona in 635 have long since vanished but the priory church and St Mary's parish church, lying on an axis with it, may be an echo of the original layout.

In the 670s Holy Island became home to St Cuthbert, one of the most revered Anglo-Saxon saints, and it was to honour him that the famous Lindisfarne Gospels were written in around 715. Vicious Viking raids began in 793 and after the raid of 875 Cuthbert's relics were evacuated from the priory and they, and the Lindisfarne bishopric, were transferred to Durham, where they remain today. The monastery was not re-established until 1093 and from then until the priory's suppression in 1537 a small community continued to occupy the site.

A local landowner, Mr Selby, acquired a lease from the Crown in the early nineteenth century and made efforts to clear and shore up the, by then, crumbling ruins. Despite this, the entire west front collapsed in the 1850s, only to be reconstructed at Crown expense. Continuing problems with maintaining the site against the North Sea winds led to the Office of Works taking it into guardianship in 1913.

St Peter's Church

Magical Saxon survival

Barton-Upon-Humber, North Lincolnshire

BY THE 940S, SAXON LANDOWNERS, with their coffers swelled by profits from their lands, increasingly began to commission their own parish churches. Many churches today have their origins as estate churches of an Anglo-Saxon landlord, which is why many parishes have boundaries that are the same as those of Saxon estates. For many Saxon landowners planning a village, building a manor house and founding a church were inextricably entwined, part of a single economic, social and religious enterprise; and the remarkable Saxon church at Barton-Upon-Humber is one such example.

It was originally built as an estate church next to a lordly fortified manor house and comprised a central tower flanked by a chancel in the east and a baptistery to the west. Like many Saxon buildings it is largely made of cut stone robbed from nearby derelict Roman buildings. The chancel and baptistery were two-storeyed and the tower had three storeys. This was not simply a place of worship, it was a symbol of the lord's status, a place for his heir to be baptised and a symbol of his local overlordship.

While the church was later much extended, the remaining Saxon part is one of the most wonderful of all the places that English Heritage cares for, and gives some sense of the intimacy and intensity of upper-class Anglo-Saxon religion. It, and the later medieval parts, were excavated by The Department of the Environment and English Heritage after they were taken into care in 1977. The excavations involved exhuming over 2,800 burials, the remains from which are now kept in the church in a special ossuary.

Battle Abbey and Battlefield

Site of the most famous event in English history

Battle, East Sussex

AFTER HIS DECISIVE VICTORY over Harold, king of the Saxons, at Battle in 1066, William the Conqueror ordered the construction of a vast abbey on the site of his triumph. The abbey church, now almost all gone, was perched on the narrow ridge upon which King Harold was slain, and the high altar was probably placed on the exact spot.

Although the church has now gone, there is plenty to see: the impressive gatehouse and courthouse still dominate the southern end of the town; the east and west sides of the cloister still stand; and the magnificent range of sub vaults beneath the monastic guest house are amongst the most impressive of their age. Standing on the abbey terraces looking across the battleground it is still possible to grasp the topography of the battle that so famously ended Saxon England and established the Normans on the throne.

After the abbey was dissolved by Henry VIII a private house was made out of the ruins, and in 1922 this was leased to a local school. Battle Abbey was requisitioned by the army following the fall of France in June 1940 and housed artillery and infantry units in temporary camps, but ater the war it resumed life as a school. In 1976 the estate was put up for sale and the Department of the Environment bought it with the aid of donations by a group of Americans who wished to commemorate the bicentenary of American independence. Thus the site of England's most famous battle was secured for the nation.

Castle Acre

Uniquely complete Norman village

King's Lynn, Norfolk

I HAVE TO DECLARE AN INTEREST: I live close to Castle Acre and my family are regular visitors. However, even if it were not for my personal geography the castle, priory and remains of the town walls would feature in the list of the most important of English Heritage's sites – indeed amongst the most important medieval sites in England.

The best way to arrive at Castle Acre is through the still-standing bailey gate of about 1200. This was the entrance to a carefully planned settlement with a castle at one end and a priory at the other. It was owned by the Warenne family who built an elegant and apparently only lightly defended house for themselves, the footings of which can still be seen. This was later incorporated into a massive defensive ring of earthworks which dominates the village today.

The priory is one of the most complete ruined monasteries in the country and one of the first of the Cluniac order. The west front of the church, remarkably still retaining its facing masonry, is perhaps the finest twelfth-century façade in England, only slightly marred by the insertion of a large fifteenth-century window. The prior's lodgings, which were later converted into a house, are the only roofed part, and in here, in an upper room, are the scarred remains of the prior's chapel with traces of original wall paintings. Elsewhere, visitors have to use their imagination to recreate the richness

The parish church, not in the care of English Heritage, is worth a visit to complete the picture of the medieval village. And importantly, the Ostrich pub is the place to have lunch!

Dover Castle

The key to England

Dover, Kent

IN THIS CHRONOLOGICAL ARRANGEMENT of the National Heritage Collection Dover could appear almost anywhere. Originally an Iron Age hill fort it was appropriated by the Romans, occupied by the Saxons, and walled in the early Middle Ages as a major fortress. It continued in active military service until after the Second World War and then was retained as a Cold War control centre. The army still has a presence and appoints a military governor.

Yet it was the Angivin Kings, Henry II, Richard, John and Henry III who created the mightiest fortress in Europe centred on the great tower – a building of enormous scale and sophistication visible in silhouette from France. These massy defences were put to the test in 1216–17 when the castle was besieged by Prince Louis of France. Successfully held, Dover was expanded in the aftermath, creating rings of concentric defences, putting it in the vanguard of European military design.

For hundreds of years the basic twelfth-century rings of fortification have been strengthened and modified, but never to such a degree that it has lost its identity as a great medieval castle. Indeed, together with the Tower of London, Windsor Castle and Edinburgh Castle, it remains one of the four great fortresses of the realm, still held by the Crown.

Between 1904 and 1908 those parts of the castle not in active use by the military were handed over to the Office of Works, and in 1930 the Great Tower was given up too. But in September 1939 everything was returned to military control. After the war buildings were gradually handed back to the Department of the Environment and only after the end of the Cold War in 1991 were the last secret underground installations transferred to English Heritage.

Rievaulx Abbey

The world's most beautiful ruined monastery

Nr Helmsley, North Yorkshire

WHEN RIEVAULX ABBEY was placed in the guardianship of the Office of Works by the Duncombe Estate in 1917 it was in a parlous state. Its walls, hung with festoons of ivy, were intensely romantic but inherently unstable. The Office of Works, led by Charles Reed Peers, excavated over 90,000 tons of fallen masonry and soil, removed a forest of vegetation and dismantled sections of walling, re-erecting them reinforced with concrete. The Office saved Rievaulx from certain collapse.

The abbey is one of a group of Cistercian foundations established in the remote valleys of Yorkshire in the early twelfth century. Three are in the care of English Heritage: Fountains, Byland and Rievaulx. These buildings experimented with new forms of architecture which today we call Early English, the first English flowering of the gothic style. Thanks to the remoteness of Rievaulx, after the dissolution of the site in 1538 the buildings were not severely plundered and so remain today amongst the earliest and most important surviving monastic structures of their date in Europe.

In 1687 the abbey became the property of Charles Duncombe, whose successors included its ruins in a vast romantic landscape centred on their new house Duncombe Park. The views of the abbey entranced travellers, painters and poets throughout the nineteenth century. None of this need be understood in detail on a visit to this magical place, for the setting of Rievaulx is still one of exceptional beauty. Here nature and artifice combine with historical and spiritual associations to create an atmosphere that never, even in the most miserable weather, disappoints.

Medieval Merchant's House

Hidden survivor

Southampton, Hampshire

A BOMB FALLING ON A BROTHEL in French Street, Southampton, in 1940, uncovered something rather unexpected. Beneath a thin modern skin the apparently ordinary building was a remarkably preserved merchant's house dating to around 1290. Southampton City Council acquired the house to protect it from further damage and after the war used it as a store for theatrical equipment.

In 1973 the council turned it over to the Department of the Environment who undertook one of the very first major reconstructions of a medieval building, trying to get all the details, including furniture, absolutely right.

The house was originally built by John Fortin, a prominent merchant. It combined residence, office, warehouse and showroom all in one. In the basement was the cellar, entered by steps from the street. Above was the merchant's shop and behind this, his great hall rising up through two storeys. At the back of the house was, perhaps, his counting house, a handsome room with carved beams and, above, bedrooms.

Today all this is revealed in the reconstruction work that took place from 1983–86, which takes the building as closely as possible back to its medieval form and appearance. This was one of the first times that English Heritage reconstructed a medieval interior for the public, starting a tradition for which the organisation is now known the world over.

Stokesay Castle

The finest thirteenth-century manor house in England

Ludlow, Shropshire

LAURENCE OF LUDLOW was a successful wool merchant who, in 1281, decided to set up as a country gentleman, buying the manor of Stokesay. Here he built a highly fashionable residence lightly fortified by a moat. His large great hall remains almost untouched, once heated by a fire burning in its centre. Great wooden shutters would have closed off the unglazed windows from the wintry gales of the Welsh marches.

At either end of the hall, blocks of buildings provided more domestic quarters. At the low end, a vertiginous stair leads up to fine chambers jettied out over the moat. At the high end, a more private great chamber led to a three-storey tower, which both provided the best accommodation and gave the house a strong castle air. From the top of this the castle's setting can be enjoyed, occupying, as it does, a strategic position in the Onny valley. The gatehouse, which was built around 1640, is one of the most exuberant timber-framed structures in a part of the country renowned for exotic framing.

Stokesay had a long history of neglect, which is why its early buildings remain unaltered. In a desperate state, it was sold by the Earl of Craven in 1869. Its new buyer was determined to save the house and spent huge sums on conserving it. But his descendants struggled to keep the building in good repair and eventually gave up, placing the castle in the care of English Heritage in 1986.

Kenilworth Castle

Spectacular medieval palace
Kenilworth, Warwickshire

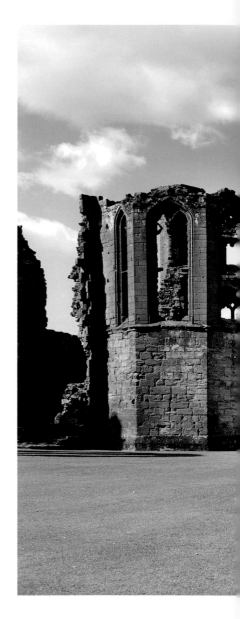

THE HISTORY OF KENILWORTH is about as illustrious as they come. In and out of royal ownership throughout the Middle Ages, it was home to some of the most significant figures in English history, including King John, Simon de Montfort, John of Gaunt and Robert Dudley, Earl of Leicester. The castle was founded in the twelfth century, and the ruined keep dates from this period, but probably the most spectacular additions were made for John of Gaunt in the 1370s.

Other than the magnificent apartments built by Edward III at Windsor Castle, John of Gaunt's palace at Kenilworth (for palace it was) was perhaps the greatest building of its age. The hall, which still stands (though unroofed), was raised up above a vaulted undercroft with spectacular views over a vast artificial lake or mere. It had five fireplaces and was lit by an early and spectacular bay window. This and the other floor- to-ceiling windows had integrated window seats and reveals filled with tracery.

Its associations with so many great figures, and in the sixteenth century with Elizabeth I, who stayed there four times, ensured the castle's fame; and Sir Walter Scott based one of his most successful novels on it. Such was the reputation of the castle that subsequent owners, right up to Lord Clarendon in the Victorian period, continued to care for and consolidate the ruins. However, eventually the costs became too great, and in 1937 the castle was bought for the nation by Sir John Siddeley, the local motor industry magnate, who placed it into the guardianship of the Commissioners of Works, with a £5,000 dowry for necessary repairs.

Lyddington Palace

Unique fifteenth-century bishop's palace

Lyddington, Leicestershire

IN THE MIDDLE AGES the wealthy bishops of Lincoln had more than a dozen residences, allowing them to tour their vast diocese and extensive landed estates. Lyddington, in Rutland, was one of their palaces – set amongst gardens, fishponds and a park. What we see today is one wing of the residence built by Bishop Alnwick (1436–1449) and embellished by his two successors.

The great hall is gone, though it was excavated in the 1970s. Now up the fine broad ceremonial stair we enter the bishop's great, or audience, chamber, vaulted with a magnificent coved timber ceiling with delicate carvings. Beyond this lies the bishop's withdrawing chamber and beyond that, a bedroom, oratory and latrine. Here you can see, like nowhere else, the way a wealthy bishop would have lived in the late Middle Ages.

In 1600 the palace became an almshouse, a use it retained until the 1930s. The buildings then remained empty and open to the elements until August 1954, when the site was officially accepted into guardianship by the Ministry of Works.

Lyddington is a very pretty village and repays a whole morning's visit to take in the church, the fishponds and the surviving medieval park pale. The pub is excellent, too.

Pendennis Castle

Britain's greatest coastal artillery fort

Falmouth, Cornwall

AFTER HENRY VIII'S BREAK with Rome people were convinced that a crusade would be launched to invade England and drag it back into the papal fold. Henry VIII ordered a massive refortification of the English coastline from East Anglia right round to Milford Haven. English Heritage has in its care several outstanding examples of this work; amongst the most important is Pendennis, which illustrates the entire history of coastal gunnery from Henry VIII's time to the Second World War.

Pendennis guards the entrance to Carrick Roads, a large natural anchorage ideal for landing an invading army. Henry VIII's artillery fort, a magnificent gunnery platform, still remains on the cliff top and a blockhouse down below. These would have devastated shipping in the water had an invading force ever materialised. Queen Elizabeth, equally worried about invasion, and perhaps with more cause, further strengthened the fort with great walls and bastions.

Pendennis did see military action, not against a foreign invader, but during the Civil War, when it became an important royalist port and stronghold. Further improvements and modernisations were made to the castle right up until 1956 when the military, who had owned the freehold since 1785, moved out and it became part of the National Heritage Collection, officially passing into guardianship in 1962.

Audley End House

England's greatest Jacobean mansion

Saffron Walden, Essex

THE REMARKABLE JACOBEAN HOUSE that stands at Audley End today is only two-thirds of the inner court of a colossus built between 1605 and 1614 by Thomas Howard, Earl of Suffolk. Howard was rapidly promoted by James I, who eventually appointed him Lord Treasurer, and it was this royal favour that spurred Howard on to build the single largest private house of the early Stuart period.

The house was so big and so lavish that Howard's successors struggled with both debt and maintenance, and eventually it was sold to King Charles II in 1666. It was not a great success as a royal palace and after 1700 it was drastically reduced in size. Yet, despite this, Audley End is one of the most magical country houses in England, retaining, despite later alterations, a strong sense of the Jacobean period.

The saloon captures the atmosphere of the state apartments, mixing the tremendous ceiling of the Earl of Suffolk's time with embellishments by his successors, who were determined to retain the rich character of the Jacobean interiors.

During the Second World War the house was requisitioned as a secret training base for the Polish resistance but in 1944 Henry Neville, 6th Baron Braybrooke, inherited the title following the death on active service of two cousins. This triggered a heavy tax liability and because the National Trust was unable to take it on due to an inadequate endowment offer, the government stepped in to buy it.

Langley Chapel

Uniquely preserved Jacobean church

Much Wenlock, Shropshire

It is REMARKABLE that the furnishings in a small chapel such as this could have survived largely untouched for 400 years. The fact that they do enables us to visualise worship in Shropshire in the reign of King James I.

The Reformation emphasis on preaching, at the expense of the Communion, led to churches being fitted with pulpits for the priest and reading desks for the parish clerk. At Langley the fine hexagonal pulpit and the rather unusual roofed reading desk still remain. For the congregation there were pews with poppy-headed finials and at the back, special desks for the musicians. Closer to the pulpit was the ornate panelled box pew used by the Lee family, the Lords of the Manor. The altar was a table and, at Langley Chapel, the monthly Communion service would have been shared like a meal, with parishioners sitting round the table on special benches. These too remain, with their kneelers and book rests.

Langley is remote today, and in the early 1600s would have been even more out-of-the-way; yet fashions in worship reached this corner of the realm, and evidence suggests that the chapel remained in weekly use until it closed in 1871. After falling into poor condition the chapel was restored in 1900 by the Society for the Protection of Ancient Buildings, and 15 years later Sir John Walter-Smyth, Lord of Acton Burnell, passed it to the Office of Works.

Boscobel House

Fifteen minutes of fame

Bishop's Wood, Shropshire

BOSCOBEL HOUSE is not a great architectural wonder; but for a few days in September 1651 it played a pivotal role in English history. It was in Boscobel woods that, after his defeat at the battle of Worcester, Prince Charles, the future Charles II, hid in an oak tree with his officer William Careless.

The nearby timber-framed farmhouse had been remodelled as a hunting lodge for a Catholic landowner John Giffard. Giffard had constructed a secret compartment in the floor of his gallery for hiding Catholic priests and it was in this cramped hole measuring only 3 feet 6 inches by 4 feet 6 inches that Charles II, over six feet tall, spent an uncomfortable night hiding from Cromwell's troops. The mound on which Charles sat the next morning and contemplated his future still stands in the garden.

These events secured Boscobel's place in history and folklore, and ever since the Restoration it has been a magnet for tourists – so much so that the original oak tree was cut away by souvenir hunters and the tree now standing was planted from an acorn harvested from the original. In 1918, following the sale of the estate to the Earl of Bradford, Boscobel's contents were dispersed. Portraits of Charles and Cromwell, and the old dining table at which Charles had reputedly eaten in 1651, were sold at auction under the heading 'a nation's heirlooms'. In 1954 the private owners, who had been opening the house to the public, placed it in the care of the Ministry of Works, who accepted it for its historical significance more than its 'intrinsic merits'. In 1988 English Heritage restored the house to its appearance in around 1900. It remains a unique and charming place that has captured the imagination of visitors for nearly 400 years.

Berwick Barracks

Early and monumental military barracks

Berwick, Northumberland

ENGLAND HAD A STANDING ARMY for the first time after the Restoration, so barracks were a new building type in the late seventeenth century. The foundations of one of the very earliest barrack blocks survives at English Heritage's Tilbury Fort, but at Berwick there remain, complete, the finest and largest barracks of the early eighteenth century.

The Glorious Revolution of 1688, which saw the replacement of the Catholic James II by the joint Protestant monarchs William and Mary, had increased security concerns on the Scottish border. The fear of Jacobite uprisings in Scotland encouraged the government to reinforce its northern fortresses and in this, the mightily fortified Berwick was a key location.

The barracks were very big and unusually pretentious, architecturally. This may have been because Nicholas Hawksmoor, one of the Office of Works' most talented architects, provided the designs. Entered through a gatehouse carrying the gilded arms of George I, the barracks on three sides enclose a parade ground. Accommodation for the troops was, by the standard of the time, comfortable: each room, lit by at least two windows and warmed by a fireplace, slept four men. Shared latrines were sited at the junction of the blocks.

The military moved out in 1963, and in recognition of the importance of the barracks, the Ministry of Works took them into care.

Chiswick House and Gardens

Cradle of English eighteenth-century aesthetics

Chiswick, London

THE BATTLE TO SAVE CHISWICK HOUSE from dereliction after the Second World War was driven in part by the fact that it was regarded as the birthplace of English Palladianism, an architectural style that was thought, at the time, to capture the essence of Englishness.

Chiswick was certainly an important place historically, and recognised as such in the 1720s when Richard Boyle, the 3rd Earl of Burlington, deployed some of his extensive fortune on creating himself a Thames-side retreat. His aim was to build a villa that an ancient Roman Senator or General might have constructed. He looked to ancient buildings he had himself seen, and to the notes and drawings of the Italian sixteenth-century architect Andrea Palladio for inspiration. The villa, built as an annexe to Boyle's adjoining Jacobean mansion, was famously described as being 'too small to live in but too large to hang on a watch chain'. It was to be hugely influential, inspiring patrons and their architects to search for purer expressions of ancient architecture.

The gardens of the villa were also intended to recreate the designed country landscapes of ancient Rome, and broke away from the rigid formality of prevailing Anglo-Dutch garden design. Together with contemporary gardens at Claremont and Stowe, the Chiswick grounds invented the English Landscape style of gardening. Known at the time as the 'natural' style of gardening, it was widely imitated in English aristocratic circles and spread into Europe and America. Today, we would not regard it as particularly 'naturalistic' but the recent major restoration of the Chiswick grounds has enabled us to enjoy the elegant, contrived informality of the gardens once again.

Goodshaw Chapel

Perfectly preserved eighteenth-century Baptist chapel

Rossendale, Lancashire

EAST LANCASHIRE was a centre of religious dissent and after 1690, when Nonconformists secured freedom of worship, many new congregations established themselves. At first these met in barns or private houses but by the 1740s purpose-built chapels were common. These buildings were normally plain utilitarian structures, partly to emphasise their difference from the parish church but also because they were erected by congregations on a tight budget.

The Goodshaw congregation was established in 1742, and in 1760 it built a new chapel using materials from an older one. The chapel remained in use until 1863, at which point it was converted into a primary school. It was this change of use that preserved its internal fittings and led to it being rescued by the Department of the Environment after it became derelict in the 1960s. The chapel was restored to its former glory by English Heritage in 1984.

The focus of the interior is the centrally placed pulpit with a sounding board above. In front of this was the singer's pew, where the choir sat, and, in front of that, was a Communion table. On the ground floor there are handsome box pews but above, in the gallery which runs around three sides, are benches. The room is still lit by a huge bronze chandelier.

The Iron Bridge

The first in the world

Ironbridge, Shropshire

VISITING IRONBRIDGE TODAY in its idyllic wooded setting it is hard to visualise this part of Shropshire as being an engine house of industrialisation. Yet shallow coal deposits made it highly attractive to ironworkers who set up their works close to the mines. In 1709 Abraham Darby I smelted local iron ore here with coke made from local coal.

The expansion of the industry was hampered by the lack of a nearby river crossing and in 1773 Thomas Pritchard, a Shrewsbury architect, came up with the idea of spanning the deep gorge with a cast-iron bridge. This was hugely ambitious in engineering terms, and at a cost of £6,000 was to prove ruinously expensive. Yet mainly using techniques adapted from timber construction, 378 tons of iron was cast into individually engineered components and assembled as a bridge. It opened in 1779 and was the first iron bridge in the world; as such it was much more than a river crossing – it was an advertisement for the technical capabilities of the Shropshire iron industry and a foretaste of advances in iron construction to come.

The bridge remained in full use for over 150 years, only finally closing to traffic in 1934, when its historic importance was recognised and it was scheduled as an ancient monument. After many years of concern about the future stability and maintenance of the structure, it was finally placed in guardianship in 1975.

Stott Park Bobbin Mill

Unique industrial survivor

Ulverston, Cumbria

IT WAS VERY UNUSUAL in the 1970s for the Ministry of Works to take into care an industrial building. The preferred route for preservation of such buildings was to establish a local trust to care for it. However, when Stott Park Bobbin Mill closed in 1971 it was immediately recognised that it should be preserved, complete with all its machinery and contents.

As its name suggests, the mill made wooden bobbins for the textile industry in Lancashire, whose need for bobbins was so great that entrepreneurs converted corn mills and even iron furnaces to satisfy the demand. The Stott Park mill was built in 1835 and was originally powered by a waterwheel fed from a mill pond. A more powerful turbine was built in 1858 and a steam engine bought in 1880 but, despite this, a combination of water and steam continued to power the mill until electric motors were introduced in 1941. None of these changes in power affected the line shafting or lathes and all the original machinery is still in situ, and active.

At its peak, the mill employed 250 men and boys and produced 250,000 bobbins a week but its fortunes were inextricably linked to the textile industry, and as this declined, and as wooden bobbins were replaced by cheaper alternatives, the mill struggled and eventually went out of business.

Kenwood House

London's great art treasure house

Hampstead, London

ALTHOUGH KENWOOD HOUSE looks, at first glance, as if it was all built at the same time, it is in fact the product of three distinct periods. The original house of about 1700 was added to by the Scottish architect Robert Adam in 1764–79. He provided William Murray, 1st Earl of Lord Mansfield, with additional bedrooms and a fantastic library. Adam encased the house in white stucco, covering over the gaps between his additions and the earlier work. The additions made in 1793–96 were in brick and provided more grand entertaining rooms. The Mansfields wanted to give the house up after the First World War and, eventually, in 1922, all Lord Mansfield's furniture and works of art were sold at auction. The house was then bought for £107,900 by the brewing magnate Edward Guinness, first Earl of Iveagh. At this stage

it was largely empty. The earl brought to Kenwood his remarkable collection of paintings, and right from the start intended to leave the whole pile to the nation. Sadly he died after only two years and so never lived at the house, which was presented to the public as a museum.

Kenwood still contains one of Robert Adam's finest London interiors – the library – but it is more famous now for the paintings by Vermeer, Rembrandt, Van Dyck and Gainsborough. The collection opened to the public in July 1928 and although amassed by Lord Iveagh had no historical link with the house before that time. Thus Kenwood is rather unusual in that there is an important house and an important art collection which cohabit. In the 1990s several rooms were redecorated, to enable the collection to be displayed more sympathetically. At the time of writing English Heritage has embarked on a project that will both enhance the display of the paintings and draw more pointed attention to some of London's most important eighteenth-century interiors.

Belsay Hall

Seminal house of the Greek revival

Belsay, Northumberland

ON HIS RETURN from an extended honeymoon in 1807 Charles Monck started to build himself a new house on his family estate at Belsay in Northumberland. Monck had been inspired by his travels in Greece and wanted to apply his knowledge of Greek buildings to create a house of the type that might have been enjoyed by the ancient Greeks themselves.

He was his own architect and the house was built from stone quarried on his own estate. This stone quarry became Belsay's hidden glory as it was transformed into a craggy rock garden that has now been fully restored.

The house, modelled on a Greek temple, is austere in the extreme. On its east side is the entrance, a severe recessed Doric portico. The entablature of this runs around the rest of the building, giving it its only external ornament. Inside, the rooms are disposed around a central atrium – the pillar hall – with two storeys of orders, the lower Ionic and the upper Doric.

The house was abandoned by the family in 1962 and by the 1970s it was riddled with dry rot, with a very uncertain future. The hall, castle and centre of the estate were taken into guardianship in 1980 and extensive repair work was begun. The terms of the guardianship mean that the house can never be refurnished and so Belsay has become the location for English Heritage's contemporary art programme.

Apsley House

The greatest and last aristocratic town palace
Hyde Park Corner, London

ALTHOUGH ARISTOCRATS had owned large London mansions from the Middle Ages, it was only in the late seventeenth century that they started to abandon their country houses and occupy these city pads for significant parts of the year. This was because of the development of the London season and the attractions and comforts of metropolitan life, which contrasted with the expense, complication and relative discomfort of living in the country. Most aristocratic town houses have now been sold and their collections dispersed; Apsley House, however, has survived to this day not only as the once town residence of the Duke of Wellington, but as the repository of his magnificent collections.

The relatively modest house built on Piccadilly in the 1770s to the designs of Robert Adam was acquired by Britain's great military hero, the first Duke of Wellington, in 1817. Under his architect Benjamin Wyatt the house was hugely extended to provide a suitable setting for the duke and his fabulous art collection. Although some of Adam's interiors survive, today the house is dominated by these additions, especially the Waterloo Gallery, the setting for the annual Waterloo banquet that was held on the battle's anniversary every year during the duke's life. This magnificent gallery, the most impressive early nineteenth-century room in London, contains the duke's collection of paintings, many from the Spanish Royal Collection.

The reason that the house and collections remained intact is due to the generosity of the 7th duke who, after the war, made over the house and most of its contents to the nation. The nation, however, treated the setting of the mansion badly. It is now marooned by busy roads and divorced from its original context. Nevertheless, Apsley House, Number One London, as it's often known, remains one of the great architectural treasures of the nation.

Osborne House

Hub of the British Empire

East Cowes, Isle of Wight

OSBORNE ALLOWS US to get extraordinarily close to Queen Victoria and Prince Albert. This was their family home, designed by Albert in the 1840s in collaboration with his builder Thomas Cubitt and his decorator Professor Ludwig Gruner. It was not what most people think of as a palace: its scale is domestic; its decoration fashionable and expensive, but not grand; its layout convenient and homely rather than overawing. Yet here the queen attended to state business and received ministers; indeed from here she ran the British Empire. So as well as the domestic there was a substantial wing for household attendants and separate accommodation blocks for the maids and the queen's Indian servants.

The royal bedrooms and nursery, all close together, reveal the close-knit intimacy of the royal family; and the extraordinary Swiss Cottage complex in the grounds, which included a museum, vegetable gardens and a miniature fort, shows the educational programme devised for the children in the summer holidays. Nearby is the private royal beach with its bathing machine set on rails, which allowed the queen to be trundled into the sea and to descend into the water with dignity and in privacy.

The death of Albert in 1861 did not bring to an end the development of the house, for as the queen's fascination with India and Indians grew she built the exotic Durbar Room in an eclectic Indian style in 1890–91. But Albert's death did usher in a morbidity at Osborne, one that to a degree still remains. The queen's bedroom, where Victoria died, is still a shrine to the Queen Empress. Locked away behind great iron gates for over 50 years, the room is now open for people to pay homage.

Berney Arms Windmill

The finest East Anglian marsh mill

Berney Arms, Norfolk

WHEN IT WAS FIRST COMPLETED in around 1865 Berney Arms Windmill could only be reached by water and, although there is now a footpath that leads there, arriving by boat is still the best and most dramatic approach. From the water the mill looks huge – it is seven storeys high, the tallest in the Norfolk and Suffolk marshlands. Its tarred brickwork contrasts strongly with the brilliant white of its cap, sails and windows.

Even after the invention of the steam engine, wind and water power remained important for many industrial processes, and not only for grinding foodstuffs. Berney Arms Mill is a case in point, for it was a cement mill. Chalk-rich clay dredged from Oulton Broad was brought here by wherry and fired in kilns, the remains of which can still be seen. The resulting clinker was brought to the mill and ground into powder as cement.

When the cement works closed in 1880 the mill was converted into a pumping station. The Norfolk and Suffolk marshes relied entirely on wind power to keep them drained, and the Berney Arms Windmill was given a scoop wheel in 1883 that lifted water out of the marshland drainage culverts and tipped it into the river Yare. It continued to perform this function right up until 1951 when the electrification of the drainage system made the mill redundant. At this point the Drainage Board agreed to present it to the Ministry of Works, who accepted it as part of a new policy to start collecting industrial monuments.

Down House

World-changing laboratory

Downe, Kent

Down House, in itself, is no architectural wonder. Like Boscobel House it was acquired by English Heritage because of its historical associations. Down was, of course, the home of Charles Darwin and the place where he wrote *On the Origin of Species* and other books.

The house, and particularly the gardens, were his laboratory, and visitors can still walk round the woodland circuit that he used when he was deliberating about his research. But it is not only a sense of the man in the context of his work that comes through, it is the man himself. Darwin was gripped by chronic medical conditions and probably a touch of hypochondria, and his study is a shrine to self-medication, as well as deep thought. His drawing room and dining room have been reconstructed and give a strong flavour of his family life.

After the Darwin family sold up in 1907, the house became a school and was then owned by a succession of institutions. None, however, could find a long term use for the house, and its condition deteriorated. In 1996, with considerable assistance from the Heritage Lottery Fund and the Wellcome Trust, Down House was purchased by English Heritage. In the years that followed it was returned to its former state, when the great man lived there.

Eltham Palace and Gardens

The best of ancient and modern

Greenwich, London

ELTHAM COULD HAVE BEEN INCLUDED much earlier in this chronological selection of English Heritage sites, for it is the largest surviving part of any medieval royal palace and has one of the greatest halls in the country. Yet it is included here as a representative of English Heritage's twentieth-century collections.

Eltham Palace was bought from the Crown Estate by Stephen and Virginia Courtauld in 1933. They commissioned the architects Seely and Paget to design them a modern house. What they designed caused a storm of controversy but is now recog-

nised as one of the most important houses of its era. Full of mod cons, like vacuum cleaners and under-floor heating, the interiors are reminiscent of the great ocean liners such as the *Queen Mary*. When complete, it was filled with Courtauld's great collection of paintings.

While the public rooms are undoubtedly impressive, it is the bedrooms that bring to life the 1930s so dramatically. Virginia's bedroom and adjoining bathroom must qualify as amongst the most evocative rooms in English Heritage's care; the vaulted ceiling and onyx-lined walls set off a marble statue of Psyche in a golden bath niche.

The Courtaulds left Eltham in 1944 and the house was occupied by army educational units until 1992 when English Heritage took over its management. English Heritage had initially planned to use the Courtauld period buildings for commercial activities. However, the restoration of the Art Deco rooms, using a combination of replica items and original pieces, was highly popular among visitors and the rooms are now open to the public most of the time.

Royal Observer Corps Bunker

Miraculous Cold War survivor

York, North Yorkshire

THE YORK BUNKER is the youngest building in the National Heritage Collection and was acquired by English Heritage almost by accident. The bunker stood in the garden of one of English Heritage's offices and only when it fell out of use in 1991 did we realise its importance. The office and garden was eventually sold in 2000 but the bunker was brought into care, ensuring the National Heritage collection continues to tell recent, as well as ancient, history.

York bunker was built in 1961 at the height of the Cold War as one of 1,561 monitoring posts designed to report the location of nuclear strikes and track clouds of radioactive fallout. Reports from the bunkers, which were manned by a volunteer corps, would be relayed to the Ministry of Defence, who could plan both military responses and civilian protection.

The York bunker is important because it uniquely retains most of its original equipment, including the Atomic Weapons Detection Recognition and Estimation of Yield Unit (or AWDREY), which would automatically trigger an alarm if an atom bomb went off within a 150-mile radius of the bunker. The most evocative part of the building is the plotting room, which retains all its situation boards, including two illuminated maps of the north of England. There are also washrooms, dormitories and kitchens, all of which provide a vivid picture of what post-holocaust life underground would have been like for the survivors. Instructions did not explain how, in the event of a strike, the occupants would be relieved or when their ordeal would end. I suspect if the worst had happened this would have become both shelter and tomb.

This edition © Scala Publishers Ltd, 2012
Text © Simon Thurley
Illustrations © English Heritage Photo Library except:
pp. 6–7 © The Boxgrove project, UCL.
p. 8 (aerial view) © Skyscan Balloon Photography/source: English Heritage
    Photo Library .
pp. 14–15 © Skyscan Balloon Photography/source: English Heritage Photo Library
pp. 46–47 © Skyscan Balloon Photography/source: English Heritage Photo Library
pp. 48–49 (interior) © Paul Highnam/source: English Heritage Photo Library

First published in 2012 by
Scala Publishers Ltd
Northburgh House
10 Northburgh Street
London EC1V 0AT
www.scalapublishers.com

In association with English Heritage
www.english-heritage.org.uk

ISBN: 978 1 85759 751 6

Editor: Sandra Pisano
Design: Nigel Soper
Printed in Malaysia

10 9 8 7 6 5 4 3 2 1

FRONT COVER:
Stonehenge
(see pp. 12–13)

FRONTISPIECE:
Boscobel House
(see pp. 52–53)

BACK COVER:
Lullingstone Roman Villa
(see pp. 20–21)